Early Echoes

❧❧

Carol Frith

FUTURECYCLE PRESS
www.futurecycle.org

Library of Congress Control Number: 2015960547

Copyright © 2016 Carol Frith
All Rights Reserved

Published by FutureCycle Press
Lexington, Kentucky, USA

ISBN 978-1-938853-97-5

Contents

The Constant Urn 7
Spring Heat 8
A City in the Heat 9
A California Childhood 10
Her Careful Mask 11
Scent of Juniper 12
Childhood—Backlit with Earring 13
Five Peonies 14
Whiskey Back 15
Decline in Time 16
Sidewalk Terrace 17
Urban Alley with No Horseman 18
Luz for Light 19
Black Orchids 20
Hagar Flowers 21
The de Sade Papers 22
Fragment Moon Pond with Closing Sapphics 24
Italian Sunflower 25
The Man in the Piano 26
Facing a Diurnal World 27
Philistines 28
Lucille in the Garden with Moonflowers 29
Free-floating Guilt 30
Tour of Nash Landscape 31
Uneasy Drift 32
Autumn Zin 33
Black Tights, a Halter Top 34
Watermarks—Walkers 35
Pinnacle of Joy 36
Basement Café 37
Wetlands 38

Long Weather.. 40
No Leaves.. 41
Voices... 42
Like a Maze... 43
I Will Wobble up a Crooked Street or Two..................... 44
Letter, Unaddressed... 46
White Bamboo.. 47
Privet Blooming.. 48
Lace-lip Orchids and a Glass Moon............................... 49
Star Jasmine... 50
Narrow Alley... 52
Random Clock.. 53
Tubular Corollas... 54
Instructing the Careless Ingenue................................... 55
Silk Thread: Transverse Obsessionals.......................... 56
Beyond the Bridge... 58
A Summer Dream.. 59
Nightmare.. 60
Indeterminate Breeze, Stone Fountain..........................61
Acknowledgments

*For my husband, Laverne,
who makes all my poems possible.*

The Constant Urn

The sirens are an early echo here,
police and fire and more, the constant urn:
the evening news a melancholy seer.

The way that sirens punctuate the year—
the dying fall—that's how the dying yearn
to rest beneath the siren's echo here.

The unimpassioned turn beyond the fear...
we scatter poison lilies, plant a fern,
the evening news, a schizophrenic seer.

Who lives? Who dies? Obsequies are unclear,
an echo's echo that we can't unlearn.
No battlefront is distant. We are here:

every prophecy too real, too near.
Forgive the prophets. Warnings crash and burn.
History rewards the manic seer,

violence reflecting in a mirror.
The seer turns his back, unmoved and stern,
the constant urn a constant echo here,
an echo of the echo of the seer.

Spring Heat

The child helps herself to this or that memory.
Yesterday, she rode the carousel in the park,

counted eucalyptus trees: bell-fruited ash,
snow gum, yellow box, and ironbark.

Too much peppermint and camphor. Today
she poses in the tulip garden, parsing

petals in the spring heat. The afternoon's
a cautious sentence, each tulip

a fountain of small color—English cultivars,
Feathering and *Flame,* unstable and unique,

some with yellow striping. Someone has
potted and replanted them, of course.

The child ignores the blossoms, still tasting
camphor from the day before.

Too many blooms and painted ponies
spoil an afternoon.

She will go inside, away from sun
and air and stringybark trees.

She will nap and dream about a gilded pony,
turning in the mallee ash,

the scent of camphor near the carousel,
the bright flesh of dying tulips

necrotic in the splendid afternoon.

A City in the Heat

Because the past is closing in. Because
I don't look back, but hurry down the street.
No shade, no plane trees. That's the way it was,
or is, because it's summer in the heat.

Because the time's so very long ago.
Because it's now. Of course the time is now.
Because you'll pass me on the left, just so,
the way you passed me then, and that is how

I'll know it's summer in the heat. And you
will smile that enigmatic way you smile.
Because you must, to make this story true.
Because I do not pause, though all the while

I hear you call from every side-street shop.
Because you turn. Because I cannot stop.

A California Childhood

She has no clue how many johns she's done.
She's stuck on daylight duty on this stroll:
a California childhood in the sun.

A squad car slows, moves on. She's not the one
he's looking for. He's not the vice patrol.
She has no clue how many johns she's done.

She hails a pickup truck. "Want some fun?"
she shouts. The driver doesn't stop. Her goal?
A California childhood in the sun.

A micro mini, heels designed to stun,
she'll pay for last night's take somebody stole.
She has no clue how many johns she's done.

She struggles with the valley heat, a run
of luck that's anything but good, the whole
unhappy truth of childhood in the sun.

A john. She hopes he doesn't have a gun.
How many minor statutes have to toll?
She has no clue how many johns she's done—
a California childhood in the sun.

Her Careful Mask

> for a girl with tattoos

She has imposed an order on herself,
a close-knit script across her breasts, her face—
lost synergies from the tattooist's shelf.
We have questions. She has answers: trace
on trace of hieroglyphs in cautious blue,
a harmony of ink, a tatted lace
of messages, some of which are true,
all of which comprise her careful mask,
a map of consequence on public view,
the woman's concept and the artist's task.
Her eyes are closed in melancholy bliss.
We hold our questions, do not dare to ask.
The ink transforms her face, a needle's kiss:
there is no pattern we can match to this.

Scent of Juniper

We came for coffee, but you ordered grapes,
and now you're reading Keats. I'm watching light
collect above the window. I brought de Sade
but haven't opened it. Across the room,

a woman of a certain age has asked
for gin. They have no liquor license here.
She settles for a latte. I see her hands
begin to shake, her skin-tight satin shirt

a bruise of lavender. I open de Sade,
a "sampler" says the promo on the back.
Justine. I'll sample that. You are lost
in *Chapman's Homer*. I sigh and try your grapes,

but I taste juniper—sad alternate
to sweetness in this uncollected light.

Childhood—Backlit with Earring

She's withdrawing her face from the mirror. A singer,
a dancer, a child. She wears a triple-hung earring:
hand-hammered silver and rubies,

her hair pulled back from her eyes. Her face, which
is purified silence, is mostly outside of the mirror.
She hasn't chosen to be here.

She sings what the chill glass has taught her, the quiet
a mist in her eyes. Reflection of hand-hammered
silver, the sound of rubies

when weeping. She has painted her face for a lover.
This one, another, another. She is drinking a wine
that consumes her,

a mercury silver that shimmers. Her veins have been
opened to back light, her childhood a fear
in the silence.

Five Peonies

Paper peonies:
saturated red—
almost black with red.
Hybrid Japanese?
Great, floppy, paper

blooms. "Five," you tell me,
"five smoky blossoms
in a smoked-glass vase."
They swallow candle-
light like burgundy.

How many glasses
of burgundy have
you and I shared? Five?
Five at minimum.
Old wine heats the tongue

and burns the careless
lips. Double hybrids—
giant fragile blooms
that trap our voices
in dusty petals,

huge and black with sound.
Light and wine and smoke
resorb the dark. In
the corner of this
room: five peonies.

Whiskey Back

She wanders past in watered silk shantung,
and suddenly it's nineteen forty-eight:
a smoky bar. The hour is growing late.
A whiskey-hearted warbler has just sung,
her pitch off-key, each note a little sprung.
The woman in shantung—she's no one's date—
stops at the bar and settles in to wait.
The bass viol's wheezing like a ruined lung.
Outside, a Hopper sign is blinking on
and off—martini olive in a glass,
brittle neon, like the blonde chanteuse.
Postwar after-hours, her gig's till dawn.
She checks the bar for clues: some jazz? some sass?
The shantung lady tips her for the blues.

Decline in Time

I listen to her voice, the way it breaks,
her laugh too brittle as she pours the wine.
She tries to hide the way her left hand shakes.

I tell the waiter that we're having steaks.
"Ah," she says, "the high life. It's a sign."
A sign that trembles in her voice. She breaks

the cautious silence with a quip that takes
an extra second to complete—decline
in time that only she would catch. She shakes

her head, smiles her rueful smile, and makes
a point of asking how I am, a line
of questioning she won't pursue. It breaks

her concentration when I pause. She fakes
a laugh, then spikes her wine with gin. "Not mine,"
I say. She hesitates, and then she shakes

her napkin out. There's something that she aches
to say, but says instead she's glad I'm fine.
I am not fine. And that's the way it breaks.
She lifts her glass. My wine glass shakes and shakes.

Sidewalk Terrace

Summer solstice afternoon, eggshell light
curving into ellipse. "It rained last night,"
you tell me. A small-veined youth pours white wine
into fluted glasses for the couple next to us.

He will bring me lukewarm coffee in a chipped mug.

I watch a crow switchback above the climbing
wisteria. I should wear opal in this light.

You tell me that your mother cultivated wisteria,
trained it on a cruciform trellis, foot-long flowering
clusters, roots tapping into slightly acid soil.

This afternoon, the gypsy musk of blooming
privet fills the air, each blossom paler than
the waiter's wrist.

"*Las gitanas,*" whispers the boy, mumbling
the corkage fee for a coast varietal.

The perfume of privet is stifling now,
like too much incense at offertory.

I listen to the traffic, a rush of air. "Like wings,"
you say. I follow the shape of your logic,
time spliced into time: random scent of
privet, pink as your mother's wisteria.

One cloud carves into the sky, off-white
wisdom of bone. "Like mother of pearl,"
you tell me, and that is my explanation.

Urban Alley with No Horseman

The door draws down to the back porch steps.
It is almost dusk or almost morning,
moon or sunlight having spilled itself
somewhere just outside the frame.

Inside the house, a lamp sheds a heartbeat
of yellow incandescence. A stray moon
is going to set (or rise) out of balance.
The sun has already gone down on its old wings.

These back porch steps are not on any
waterfront; no sea and no lax tide push
against inky rocks. You and I have lived
in this dream: low alders or bushes in the alley.
No stately plane trees and not a single linden.

In this narrow alley there is no horseman.

Tonight, you tell me that you see looping
eucalyptus and a solitary moon, some kind
of path, or maybe none, an enchanted forest
that has nothing to do with dawn or dusk
falling or rising in this alley that is nowhere
near the sea, no horseman whatsoever waiting
moon-drunk and solitary on a weed-green
paving stone to celebrate the kind
of light that's not even here
behind this sad brick house.

Luz for Light

You tell me something is uneven here,
gets lost in the translation. *Hacedor,*
the maker. Or *miedo,* which is fear.

A certain rapture in the written score.
Moon in autumn, white as *huesos:* bone.
La luna; I can't see it anymore.

You tell me passion's in the undertone,
and I forget to listen, cold as moon-
light in the garden of my *corazón:*

My heart grows quiet by the afternoon,
the garden *blanca y sagrada,* white
with shifted sunlight. *La luz* will dim too soon,

you say. My close translation learns to write
itself, the text transcribing *luz* for light.

Black Orchids

You tell me memory is syncretic.
That's William James, "weakening the image,"
recollection becoming its own topic.

I want to take up breeding orchids—false
semi-albas. I picture cognate blossoms,
my images a kind of agitation in the lamplight.

You connect my words like beads in a rosary,
each bead a dot, each dot a blossom—sepals
in a greenhouse. I'm feeling short of breath.

I can hold an entire hothouse in my palm,
chromatics fading in and out. Have I just told
you that? James' "pure experience," no doubt.

And now, an unremembered cymbidium
is swallowing my lamplight. You tell me
memory's a coax, a tease. I shall raise amber

orchids, each petal like bruised flesh.
I remember bruises but forget the injury,
synapse to purple synapse, subtle—

curative as an electrical storm. I have
forgotten entire greenhouses—a kind
of Jamesian tension—and remembered one

black orchid. I shall reconstruct a whole
decade of such blooms, one black petal
at a time.

Hagar Flowers

You tell me women turn their backs,
forget themselves. I tell you that
morning glories have climbed
the fence across the alley.
I saw the blossoms just today,
lupine-colored blooms in the early
heat. I have rested all morning
in their lavender shade.

Morning glories…Hagar flowers
sent to bloom here and where,
I cannot say.

You're not interested in the
blossoms on these vines.
You'll prune them back tomorrow.

"Destructive to the fencing stakes,"
you will say, and I won't
disagree.

I wait for further commentary,
but you turn to go inside.
I remain here, in the margin
of ragged grass at the edge
of the alleyway, to watch
the crumbling afternoon
take on the color of closing
morning glories.

THE DE SADE PAPERS

Lune, la lune—this much moonlight.
There is no moon.

The sprinkler is running at the rental house
and, in the scalding sunlight of the Central Valley,
I am reading de Sade: *Philosophy in the Boudoir.*

Like Rilke's angel, let me be astonished here—
bright azaleas wilting in the sun.

I've been unwell—pneumonia, and the heat
is feverish. I dreamed last night of Charenton,
The 120 Days of Sodom. I want to wake up
in someone else's dream.

The sprinkler circles, cascading water through
the drought. I'll read some Rilke next—elegies
and careful gardens that settle into a lament.

But today it's de Sade, the air around me
tight as sealed glass. What emerges from
this heat is focus.

De Sade and Latour were imprisoned at Miolans.
De Sade could have channeled Orpheus
and walked away, looking backward
once or twice—negative lessons
in the vacant passion of his light.
Or, he could have taken Latour, escaped
across a blood-dark sea. He did neither.

My garden hose is arcing wildly in the sun
now, spinning drought out of the azaleas
and the agapanthus. I move the sprinklers
to the desiccated redwood tree.

In this viral heat, I turn the page, begin to read
from *Crimes of Passion.*

Fragment Moon Pond with Closing Sapphics

Her ornamental pond is lined with shards—
bitumen pottery that she fired last winter

during long-night's moon. In May, she
shattered the work of her wheel.

Her summer pool is a gesture, a jagged
bowl depressing the soil.

It is red moon now, high summer. Water
lilies fill the pond, fragrant night-

blooming pink-shells. The water at midnight
is seventy degrees.

The moon itself is fluid. Jagged shards
line the lily pool—

the shards she has broken with her hands;
they move up to her now, through the shadows.

Fragile darkness, damaged with lilies, and her
song rehearses meters in shattered Sapphics:

"Red moon. Hands of summer. Oh, bruised the lilies.
Broken the moon pond."

Italian Sunflower

A white Italian sunflower in a vase;
gravid spirals circle, opening
the disc florets. Infertile petal rays

surround the center in a shaggy maze
of random art, almost disordering
this white Italian sunflower in a vase.

I've spent the morning in a random haze,
watched uncertain light diminishing
the disc florets, the sterile petal rays—

a shadow and a shadow's dark bouquets.
Outside, a mating wren begins to sing,
the careful sunflower blooming in its vase—

small purpose in a half-linked chain of days.
I take whatever gifts the shadows bring,
the disc florets, the sterile petal rays,

a season entering its blooming phase,
the ache of Sunday morning shadowing
the white Italian sunflower in a vase,
its disc florets, its barren petal rays.

The Man in the Piano

He gathers words in the palm of his right
hand, closing them in with his left. (I mean to say
he makes a double fist.) He knows language
can catch in the piano, tangle in the underlever
leads and damper wires, trip over the *balancier*
and repetition springs.

He uses language like a soundboard,
the head of a drum. "Sprucewood,"
he says, a slow output he opts not to hear.

He is listening for pain, for the elevated concept
of form. He matches notion after notion
of tone—transverse vibrations. Independent
of the piano's springs, bridges, and ribs,
he doesn't know who he is.

In this dark air, he will not touch a key or balance-
pin. He is tone-on-tone invisible in
the abrupt dark. His voice drones on, balances
the tuning pins, the string-rest felt, the sharps.

It is night beneath the key coverings.
He will not find morning.

Facing a Diurnal World

The day opens past an edge of light,
too much light, catching on the corner
of my vision, opening a blindness,

sunrise wobbling as I look east
out of the long uncertainty of dark,
the sun coming up on an edge of light,

impervious to sunglasses or shadow,
random explosions of light overpowering
my vision, opening a blindness:

new edge of blind light, and I have
appointments in cities beyond the glare
of this turning edge of sunrise, beyond

these strobe lights flashing up out
of dawn, this white-hot cascade that
opens an aura like blindness.

I want to turn from the window,
to wait for quiet, for darkness, for
the last cataract of daylight to fall
down from the edge of the world.

Philistines

>after *Philistines* by George Andreas

I am walking on my heels through the sand to avoid
the Philistines, looking backward over my shoulder.
They should or shouldn't be here.

Nonetheless, they babble and fuss in their oh-so-public
syntax. They haunt each other with their punitive
little hands, vertical and sour as Byzantine saints.

In this rose-red landscape, there are no trees.
The sky is blue with the sick anxiety of heat.

The narrow Philistines—there are three
or four of them—smile and move like phantoms
behind me, lounging like common thieves when
I turn quickly to face them.

There is so much left for them to say.
Very soon these dark hills will stop
like a red clock.

The narrow Philistines will call and call
to each other and whisper, and I will have
to believe all of this, no matter how red
the earth is, how very blue the useless,
overhanging sky.

Lucille in the Garden with Moonflowers

Lucille is watering the moonflowers in the garden
after dark. Night after night, it's the same:
petals like white fire, incense of too many years,

each flower's face pale on the random vines,
fragrant sepals on the powdery edge of light—
Lucille, watering the moonflowers in the garden.

The vines cover her garden wall, overgrow
the fence, night-blooming and wine-sweet,
petals like white fire, the incense of too many years.

The moon is gibbous now and waxing. Lucille
explores each vine for seed pods throbbing in the dark,
watering the moonflowers in her garden,

each jade leaf moistened with a glaze of white mist.
In the palm of her hand, she shelters petals as if they
were white fire, the incense of so many of her years.

She raises moonflowers, nighttime cousin of
the morning glory, dying back each fall,
Lucille in the garden watering each burning flower,
petals like the white-fire incense of too many years.

Free-floating Guilt

The air's unquiet—not wind so much as breeze,
a breeze that whispers rumors in my ear—
accusatory tales. The wind's a tease,

although it isn't really wind I hear
but grievances—and vague, free-floating guilt.
I hum a little song outside of fear,

though I am not afraid. What I have built,
I've built—a patchwork kind of wild-rose song.
I watch noon roses fade, and soon they'll wilt.

Music. Fading blooms. I can't go wrong.
I relish how the light of summer thins
and how this wild-rose reverie grows long.

And now I hear accusing violins
keening forth the music of my sins.

Tour of Nash Landscape

after Landscape from a Dream *by Paul Nash*

We shall return by way of the five-piece
glass panel. Notice how the dark head-
land forms a semilagoon where waves crease
the gray sand into linear dunes. Instead
of navigating by compass—the sun's still up—
we'll find our way back by shadows the panel
frames cast on the sand, a kind of map,
the lines of which are not quite parallel.
Note them, please. We shall be passing through
the painting? mirror? window? in a moment,
past the self-reflective eagle, into
a salmon-colored sunset, radiant
with stones and clouds and raptor shadow. One
by one, let's walk now into that sad red sun.

Uneasy Drift

A nervous wind this morning. Across the street
the neighbor's restless willow stains the grass
with troubled shade. No more August heat.
The twelve-hour light is brittle as old glass:

autumnal equinox. An even day
for now, but it's intending to be less…
familiar old diminishment. A spray
of notes—somebody's wind chimes I would guess—

filters down the block, a blue-green shift
of breeze that echoes with an underlilt
of musical malaise, uneasy drift
of sound: wind song with an edge of guilt.

Lost season, willow branches trailing in
the wind. Time's uneven discipline.

Autumn Zin

There is one daylight moon. I see two,
a double image. And now you tell me there is
someone by the gate, a man. I put down my glass
of autumn wine.

Most of the trees in our backyard have lost
their leaves. I track this story on the rim
of my glass.

I am older now; I shall wear black lace.

There he is again—the man by the back gate.
I raise my arm to point. You refill my glass
with Zin.

You've found a flower. Narcissus? Ivory petals
with a bright red center. Strange to find it now,
in autumn. Narcissus bloom in the spring.

I watch the afternoon light being absorbed into
the petals of the out-of-season narcissus,
its heart pulsing blood-red in the blank sun.

"*Sangre,*" whispers the man at the gate, "*Sangre.*"

Sensory anesthesia: I had ceased to feel his
presence. "Let him in," I tell you.

You're moving toward the gate, but he is gone.
You pluck the lone narcissus and drop it in my glass.
Its pale narcotic tracks amnesia in the Zin.

Black Tights, a Halter Top

She's waiting near the corner of Monroe
and Pierce: spike heels, black tights, a halter top,
her image coding sunlight. Who will stop,
eclipse this smolder that is burning slow
as incense on the walk? Is she a pro?
Perhaps, although a slowly cruising cop
on Pierce ignores her. Her cigarette's a prop.
She never takes a drag—a cameo
against the sun, her small face smiling at
whatever thing it is might fill her needs.
Two sparrows? The donut shop across the street?
At her back, an oak. The light is flat.
Pinned to the tree, a ragged sign that reads:
"For Sale. Persimmons, firm to the touch, and sweet."

WATERMARKS—WALKERS

I.

Late afternoon with umbrellas: impermanent
watermarks. Men and women walk outside them-
selves in careful rain. I place my palm against
the surface of this watery light, more rain than

these walkers will ever need, paths of drenched air
between them, umbrellas like bubbles, like cut flowers,
lenses of wet light blue as ripe plums, water
passing through a liquid rise of air.

II.

Reverent walkers fold their hands and bow
into the water, each figure a compartment of fierce
absence, the mind in rain a closed maneuver.
At the bottom of the afternoon, fruit and flowers,

blue and green confusions, the air like wet glass.
I cannot see a single human face, the air whining
at an uncertain pitch. In rain the light is always
waiting, cautious as these square penitents troubling

their umbrellas, moving the way light has learned
to move through water, door of rain too wide,
too square, too quiet, and it does not close.

Pinnacle of Joy

after *Seated Man* by Peter Max

You sit here like a wish for something incomplete.
Beside you, tulips in a pepper pot
turn inside out, your bowler hat erasing
hours of time: the blank idea of it,
its special privacy—your cultish tie
tucked down beneath your waistcoat.

And now I dream you into order
on the white slats of your chair; I look
into you like the sun, your face intractable,
a wash of mauve light.

You are at this moment the only man
in this room, a peach-blossom
glow above your head, your wandering
gaze a self-sufficient spell.

You are untrustworthy, your attitudes
uneven, but I so admire your tie,
your blue side tables.

Together, we listen to the traffic noise.
Neither one of us is startled—it is a deep
sound, clear as water that may or may not
be filling up the pepper pot on your left.

In this orderly room your distinct eyebrows
verge on structure; they break my heart,
your bee-sting mouth a rosy pinnacle of joy.

Basement Café

A quarter of a stairwell down, yellow
incandescent light, a creaking jukebox.

Why do I remember this? Decades have passed.
There is no gravel alleyway now,
no basement café, no grass bordering
the gravel that is no longer there.

Down that vanished stairwell, a confusion of light—
acrid incense of tobacco smoke, light filtering
to the ceiling: memory's light.

I was there alone. I'm sure I ordered something.
I must have ordered...
darkness collecting in the alleyway outside.

I overstayed. That much I'm certain of: the busboy
anxious, the waitress long since gone home.

When I left, I drifted through the fog,
keeping loner's time, uncharting decades,
some part of me still caught there.

Café El Rancho. Supper underground.
I cannot tell you when—except that I was young.
Time has its limitations. And its quiet seconds run.

Wetlands

White fog steams
from the fallow wheat field.
We have left the car to walk
along the margin of this shallow stream
past shore willows, stunted and leafless,
gone to root. A sandhill crane
flushes from the path ahead of us,
cradles at the horizon, and disappears.

I want to tell you that the air is harmless,
but I don't know what that means.
The winter stream is brackish, almost black.

You examine the lichen
on an injured cottonwood, talk to me
about valley elderberry
and endangered brush rabbits.

The fog diminishes. A thin, winter sunburst
shocks our eyes. It rained last night—
puddles shine like wet redemption
in the wheat fields. You tell me
we are hungry for this light.

I watch it gleam across the roost ponds,
glow on an Aleutian goose,
dead in the drowned marsh grass,
a sad decay. Avian cholera, you say.

I shiver in the cold geometric of the sun's glare.

In the skyward eye of the motionless goose,
a purple iridescence dies over and over
into the shattering light.

Long Weather

These are your streets, my friend, a minor village
on a fog-drenched sound, the cold wail of cypress
up the coast. Broken sailboats list in the light.

I imagine you moving through narrow alleys,
scattering shadows, heels clicking on cobblestones.
These are your streets, your minor village

filled with Cézanne light. You are breathing
darkness in that light, walking to the end of the street.
Up the coast, the broken sailboats pitch and list.

Your purpose is the clean shift of motion, walking
past me always. I do not have your compass.
These streets are yours, and this is your village.

You are lost inside the geography of your own
careful movement. All geography is lost.
Up the coast, sailboats list in just this light.

You know the damage of long weather. You claim
you are not lost. Your own route is always another—
through your streets, inside your minor village...
up the coast where sailboats list in their own light.

No Leaves

It's winter. There's a rime of frost along
the eaves. I'd rather not go out today.
I dread the silence and the chill. That's wrong.
It's not silent. A solitary jay,
complaining of the cold, has settled on
the gate. I step outside reluctantly.
Autumn and its saffron light are gone.
The jay, who flutters to the maple tree,
continues his lament. "No leaves," he seems
to say, "no leaves." No shelter. I understand
the way bright winter air can chill the dreams,
can shake the body with a frigid hand.
My empathy is wasted. The jay has flown.
I'm stranded in this diamond light, alone.

Voices

When I think of how we're laid to rest,
when I remember how the songs begin
to sing themselves, the voices weaving in
the dark along the walls, the children dressed
for Sunday—band of frightened angels blest
with "Voices that Divide the Sky," sin
and fans dividing "Savior" from a thin
rendition of "Abide with Me"...obsessed
with hymns in parts, I know the way that I
will lay it down—with gospel's steady breath:
"Asleep in Jesus" and "A Few More Years
Shall Roll," shape-note parts that sanctify
the prayers: "Sweet Hour," sweet years, sweet mother death,
the witnessing, the singing and the tears.

Like a Maze

Too much to do, too much to think about,
and I succumb to careless apathy.
The hours are like a maze with no way out.
I'd like a change, a bit of mystery,
a tryst with time down empty corridors,
the naked glare of incandescent light
on aging carpet tacked to softwood floors.
The decades pass me by like so much sleight
of hand. I'd like to realign the clock,
relive a day or two: a dark café,
a rented room, a door, an antique lock
to which there is no key. I'd like to say
the corridors are empty halls I've crossed
and crossed. I'd like to say I am not lost.

I Will Wobble up a Crooked Street or Two

I will leave by the French doors,
stopping only for minor landmarks:
salty shadows, for example, underneath
a desert tamarack tree.

I will take no provisions; I will grow lean,
living off my own flesh.

I will walk through midnight and make a point
of carrying several afternoons in my backpack.

Blind apple, aspen, and pecan:
I will wait often in the shade of trees.
I can be anywhere. January, for example,
or May.

Pine, cottonwood, sycamore, willow:
I will count sidewalks in Taos

and likely stop over in several places
for the translucent, missing faces
of people I have loved.

In small towns, I'll wait by dovecotes,
write my journey down on dressed stone.

Some doors open wide, and some
open just a crack. I will depart.

I will journey to the ocean, seas away
from the closed circle of here:

Seattle's Pacific, South China's Sea, or
New York's black Atlantic.

I'll compare the dip and roar of tides,
bathe in the waters of swell and rush.
I will breathe seawater foam.
I will eat stars.

Letter, Unaddressed

The sycamores have grown a bit since you left.
Their dry leaves rasp in the heat. On the corner,
the Ruiz Market still sells sandwiches and coffee
at lunchtime, although the Ruizes have been
gone for years.

It's very warm this evening. The red paint
we carefully applied to the front porch is
peeling now. Remember the box turtle we found
after that heavy March rain? I never see
turtles anymore.

This evening, I'll water the acanthus and
the baby's tears. Across the street, unpruned
wisteria festoons Aggie's porch.

Barn owls still live in her palm tree.
That blowsy yellow cabbage rose
you planted over by the cherry tree
is putting out canes this spring,
but it doesn't bloom anymore,
no longer litters the lawn with
its bright fleshy petals.

The evening light is coming down now,
thick with lavender. Were I to photograph
this street, I'd use a broken lens.

White Bamboo

You ask if I recall the house—south of the park—
its front lawn a forest of white bamboo.
You're reading Ming poetry in translation. I want

to plant a willow tree: equations of disagreement.
I tell you that the willow is jade green, rich beads
of color, like the bracelet that you gave me once.

You are finished with willows, have moved on
to bamboo. A small shade reconfigures itself
in my imagination. "Acute nature," you say.

I misunderstand this to be Confucianist,
but you correct me. Memories of bamboo,
white as willow bark: I try to hold these images

in my mind. You read a poem or two of praise.
"Texts," I say. "Nothing but texts."
And now you talk to me about the festival

of lanterns, read me *shih* poems and regulated
verse—a music somewhere that I cannot hear.
I listen instead to late frogs in the solstice heat.

The willow tree I will not plant is greener
than the jade I wear now at my wrist.
How many beads of color do I count?

Privet Blooming

From the window, the scent of privet blooming.
Two candlesticks on the old, marble-top clock.

The poppy-bright scent of privet is heavy as
poison, the air unreadable.

This is altogether too intense. I pour a glass
of wine, the decanter leaking lead
solutes into my merlot.

Everything unmakes its small cologne.
On the wall, a mural-print, human

images, peculiar end-stopped balloons
for faces and, for breasts, more balloons:
a sextuple pattern, each balloon

fat as a wine grape curing in slow heat.
The grapes are behind a row of poplars—

no, they are behind the privets—blooming
with a thick white floral. I will remember
what I please: the scent of spiced gravities,
a kiss of privet, overheating the air.

Lace-lip Orchids and a Glass Moon

Black linen sheets, black linen curtains: the spiral
nude who lives in this room is turning
like a glass wheel: let her axis equal x.

Outside, a gibbous moon rises, rolling like an off-
center marble. The nude has never seen herself
beyond these non-equiangular ellipses.

She will wake up spinning through her skin's
inflorescence. The light that is not in this room
shatters like black glass around her slack,

spiral breasts. Imagine how extrinsic the dark
sky is—the same night, over and over again.
The nude dreams of lace-lip orchids circling

her body, the smoky glass room in which
she almost sleeps capturing every word she has
not uttered. Intrinsic equation: nude at axis x,

turning in the brittle dark. Through
the window, the blank moon, underexposed,
rolls like a great glass eye.

STAR JASMINE

This much I will fill with color: a five-point
star jasmine on the fence, morning glories
in bloom, vines green as emeralds.

The year moves itself forward. Nothing vanishes.
Everything accords with everything.
I tell you that I want a clavier.

You, of course, prefer the piano. I think in
sound bites: a clavier resting on a tied-silk
carpet, music by the separational clock.

Pianos, I try to tell you, presuppose the clavier.
The wind is coming up. I imagine myself
in a small glass cell, channeling Coleridge with
my singular silk carpet and my clavier:
Coleridge in tight, concentric circles of pattern
with too much green.

Sound is latent. I count out senses
for you: one, two, three….

We will grow old parsing syllables. We have had
our ceremonies—and walked away from them
in circles.

Last winter, we killed the jasmine bees
in their hive. They were weakening
the structure of the fence. All love
is measured.

About the clavier: I want you to understand.
When I was a child, my family outran
a hurricane blowing from the Gulf.
The sky inverted over us like a dark green cup.

On my clavier, I will place a single wilted tulip,
dying absolutely scarlet into all that out-
distanced green.

Narrow Alley

I've spent a long evening in this café.
The solitary incandescent light ignores me.
No morning glories, no ivy, no English roses

here. My aging booth is upholstered in red
plastic, and it's splitting. No one's at the counter.
I've spent a long evening in this café,

trying to remember what it seems I've
half-forgotten—some scene that I recall
with morning glories, ivy, English roses.

I'd like a glass of wine for reminiscence,
but all they serve here is coffee, and it's bitter.
I'm losing track of time in this café.

Where was that garden? Were there hollyhocks?
My life's become a memory of memories—
climbing ivy, morning glories, English roses,

some narrow garden off a narrow alley
that I almost know but, then again, I don't. And so
I spend another evening misremembering the dark:
no morning glories, no ivy, no English roses.

Random Clock

I'll cast my vote for random timelessness,
no careful schedules that I'm forced to meet,
no email headaches and no cell-phone stress.

I'm tired of sidewalks with too many feet,
and how can anybody meditate
with all those horns and sirens in the street?

I find it hard enough to navigate
my way through all life's irritating woes.
A little peace will help me concentrate

on simple pleasures like a garden rose
or sunny days with shade. I will lock
my cares away beneath my winter clothes.

The moment's come to take up taking stock,
reset the ticking of the timeless clock.

Tubular Corollas

I have stood more than once at this window,
blank-faced, a cautious woman. I want to think
about the way a moment catches beneath a daylight
moon, to wear flowers in my hat, violet
penstemon—how difficult they are in such
a use. I prefer a tubular corolla, *P. digitalis* for
the way it holds its seeds: foxglove, penstemon,
figwort—white or lavender to slow a case
of tachycardia. Pale hairy beardtongue,
digitalis flowering in an open field, purple
harvest for a roiling heart. But I am
inside, looking out—no hat, no flowers,
and no disk of daylight moon, swimming like
a spangled fish above a field of foxglove.

Instructing the Careless Ingenue

a madrigal after Virginia Woolf

Life is windowless. Lay down the sky
in quiet shades. Lay down the color blue,
divided, unobtrusive, just off-true,

the blue, perhaps, of watered silk. Now, lie...
to unconvince the careless ingenue
that life is windowless. Lay down the sky
in quiet shades, so much cautious blue.

Teach the careless ingenue to try
to comprehend that life is clue on clue
on clue, with only watered silk for view,
that life is windowless. Lay down the sky
in quiet shades. Lay down the cautious blue,
divided, unobtrusive, just off-true.

Silk Thread: Transverse Obsessionals

Whisper of white mulberry—one continuous
filament. The silk moth—*Bombyx mori*—
flightless and blind.

Tonight, the slender light of late evening,
late June. No *Bombyx mori* here.

This light is the only thread of its only source,
unbleached and half discolored.

I have spent whole seasons ill and unreasoning,
obsessed with the silver weight of close-spun
bobbin thread,

refined pigments, gold dust, tinfoil
to mimic silver tarnishing to shadow.

You beg me to leave shadow
for a skein of disorderly light, spun whole,
spun in darkness.

Wild threads from wild silk:
broken...mineralized...unraveling.
A thin, unmeasured thread
rebalancing.
A thread to be woven into itself.

"Into itself," I repeat, the way silk is woven
on handlooms by Thai women.
Woven out of threads at right angles to the dark,

raw silk's seamless whisper against the skin,
against the light—whisper of white
mulberry: one continuous
obsessional thread.

Beyond the Bridge

Sausalito and its daybreak lung of sky—
bearberry manzanita and delphiniums.
Above the beach, a lone calypso orchid.

Silence now, words pieced together
without sound, a half-song, air stretched
blue as the bone china coffee cup
you held that day.

Years telescope in the light: iris the color
that your eyes were then, the air like silk.

"Help me count the gulls," you said, the great,
white ocean breathing into sky: California gulls,
Western gulls, Heerman's gulls.

"I'm not undisciplined," you told me carefully, but,
of course, my friend, we were.

Meaning shifts with the salty light. You held
the ocean to my ear that day like a shell.

If I were to look up this afternoon, there would
be gulls. I do not look up.

A Summer Dream

The foxing parchment of a memory:
we're smoothing linens on the unmade bed.
I dream a summer moon, three sails, the sea.

Whose summer is it? This part is lost to me—
or vague. Perhaps the moon's a sun. I spread
the foxing parchment of this memory—

pale vellum—on the bed. It's utterly
invisible to you. Some shadow's fed
this dream of mine: a moon, three sails, the sea.

You fold a quilt with patient sympathy.
Perhaps the dream is something that I've read:
the foxing parchment of a memory

that isn't even mine. Two or three—
what are they—sails? I hear what you have said:
I dreamed the summer moon, the sails, the sea.

We stack the dirty linen. Nothing's free.
You ask me if my moonlight-ships have fled.
I close my eyes to save this memory,
my summer dream: red moon, three sails, one sea.

Nightmare

I am running. The past is in darkness,
a late rain reflecting in the street, the shadow
of a house looming like a ghost carousel.

Yesterday, the air was like velvet, Lenten
purple with a soporific light. But not now. Now
I am asleep and running through my life,

through darkness, running parallel to a wrought-
iron fence. I hear a low cry—a carney barker,
perhaps—calling from the shadowy house

that continues to turn aimlessly in the lees
of someone else's life. This is not my dream.
I am running through the rainy dark

out of my own past. I will not wake up in the
velvet light of this year's Lent. A distant Wurlitzer
cranks out a barcarole from the noir house.

I have never lived here. The street is smoke
and shadow, the light wet and sourceless. I am
running out of my own life into a stranger's dark
present, my lost past ticking like a broken carousel.

Indeterminate Breeze, Stone Fountain

I have separated myself from the letters
of the alphabet, from the stone fountain
in the neighbor's yard.

I have forgotten what it is I need to know,
what mysteries I need to listen for.

I will parse the sentence of the afternoon,
each word drifting like a frail leaf
on an indeterminate breeze.

Were my French good enough,
I would translate my unrest into
perfectly modulated French phrases.

My French is no longer good at all.

I shall put aside my small book and think
of how long I have lived my life in youth.
In age.

I shall wear a warm scarf and contemplate
the passage of the quiet years.

I shall put on a modest dress and walk
the neighborhood, counting pairs of courting
flickers in the tulip trees.

I shall focus on the clean beauty of time
in its increase and time in its diminishment.

I shall face the east to say my daily prayers.
I shall walk until the evening turns to stone.

Acknowledgments

These poems or versions thereof have appeared in the following publications:

AEI Festival Program: "Indeterminate Breeze, Stone Fountain"
Abbey: "Autumn Zin"
Atlanta Review: "I Will Wobble up a Crooked Street or Two," "Whiskey Back"
CFCP, Inc., Prizewinning Poems: "Long Weather," "Watermarks— Walkers," "Italian Sunflower," "Nightmare"
Chaffin Journal: "Tour of Nash Landscape"
Common Ground Review: "A City in the Heat," "Pinnacle of Joy," "Star Jasmine"
Cyclamens and Swords: "Tubular Corollas"
Darkling Magazine: "Five Peonies," "Sidewalk Terrace"
Freshwater: "Hagar Flowers"
Iodine Poetry Journal: "The Man in the Piano"
Rattle: "Black Tights, a Halter Top"
RHINO Poetry: "Philistines"
Ship of Fools: "Lucille in the Garden with Moonflowers"
Song of the San Joaquin: "A Summer Dream," "No Leaves"
The Country Dog Review: "Urban Alley with No Horseman"
The King's English: "Scent of Juniper"
The Lyric: "Her Careful Mask," "Like a Maze," "*Luz* for Light," "Voices"
Tiger's Eye: "Black Orchids," "Fragment Moon Pond with Closing Sapphics," "Letter, Unaddressed"
Timber Creek Review: "White Bamboo"
WomenArts Quarterly Journal: "Privet Blooming"

Cover photo and author photo by Laverne Frith; cover design, photo treatment, and interior book design by Diane Kistner; Overlock text and titling

About FutureCycle Press

FutureCycle Press is dedicated to publishing lasting English-language poetry books, chapbooks, and anthologies in both print-on-demand and ebook formats. Founded in 2007 by long-time independent editor/publishers and partners Diane Kistner and Robert S. King, the press incorporated as a nonprofit in 2012. A number of our editors are distinguished poets and writers in their own right, and we have been actively involved in the small press movement going back to the early seventies.

The FutureCycle Poetry Book Prize and honorarium is awarded annually for the best full-length volume of poetry we publish in a calendar year. Introduced in 2013, our Good Works projects are anthologies devoted to issues of universal significance, with all proceeds donated to a related worthy cause. Our Selected Poems series highlights contemporary poets with a substantial body of work to their credit; with this series we strive to resurrect work that has had limited distribution and is now out of print.

We are dedicated to giving all of the authors we publish the care their work deserves, making our catalog of titles the most diverse and distinguished it can be, and paying forward any earnings to fund more great books.

We've learned a few things about independent publishing over the years. We've also evolved a unique, resilient publishing model that allows us to focus mainly on vetting and preserving for posterity the most books of exceptional quality without becoming overwhelmed with bookkeeping and mailing, fundraising activities, or taxing editorial and production "bubbles." To find out more about what we are doing, come see us at www.futurecycle.org.

The FutureCycle Poetry Book Prize

All full-length volumes of poetry published by FutureCycle Press in each calendar year are considered for the annual FutureCycle Poetry Book Prize. This allows us to consider each submission on its own merits, outside of the context of a contest. Too, the judges see the finished book, which will have benefitted from the beautiful book design and strong editorial gloss we are known for.

The book ranked the best in judging is announced as the prize-winner in the subsequent year. There is no fixed monetary award; instead, the winning poet receives an honorarium of 20% of the total net royalties from all poetry books and chapbooks the press sold online in the year the winning book was published. The winner is also accorded the honor of being on the panel of judges for the next year's competition; all judges receive copies of all contending books to keep for their personal library.

www.ingramcontent.com/pod-product-compliance
Lightning Source LLC
LaVergne TN
LVHW020939090426
835512LV00020B/3428